Interview
with a KANGAROO
& Other Marsupials Too

Written by
Andy Seed

Illustrated by
Nick East

WELBECK

Published in 2022 by Welbeck Children's Books
An imprint of Welbeck Children's Limited, part of Welbeck Publishing Group.
Based in London and Sydney
www.welbeckpublishing.com

Design and layout © Welbeck Children's Limited
Text © Andy Seed 2022
Illustrations © Nick East 2022

Designer: Sam James
Associate Publisher: Laura Knowles
Editor: Jenni Lazell

FSC
www.fsc.org
MIX
Paper from
responsible sources
FSC® C020056

ISBN 978-1-78312-856-3

Printed in Heshan, China

10 9 8 7 6 5 4 3 2 1

Contents

Introduction

Well, after interviewing a big growly tiger and a huge bitey shark for the first two books in this series, I decided to go for something a little more friendly and bouncy this time. You can't get a beast with much more BOING than a kangaroo, so that is where I started!

I also wanted to talk to something CUTE and CUDDLY. And that's when I discovered that Australia is full of these gorgeous animals called MARSUPIALS. So I talked to the sweet koala and the funny wombat and discovered that these animals have POUCHES. Well, all except one.

But then I interviewed some more marsupials and found out that they don't all live in Australia, either! And lots of them have really wacky names like "quokka" and "bandicoot" and "cuscus!" Plus, not all marsupials are gentle and cuddly–there's a thing called the Tasmanian devil. Do not ask for one of those as a pet! (Well, unless your sister is REALLY annoying.)

Oh wait, hang on, you want to know how I can talk to animals? Well, easy! I invented the TRANIMALATOR–a machine to turn yaps, squawks, and howls into words. Ha, clever me!

So only read this book if you can put up with animals that are sometimes RUDE, SILLY, SNARLY, NERVOUS, AMAZING, STRANGE, and CLEVER. You have been warned . . .

Interview with a
Red Kangaroo

Here is one of the bounciest beasts on the planet. He's from Australia, he has ENORMOUS feet, he's the largest marsupial of them all, and a wallaby he is NOT . . . It's the mighty RED KANGAROO!

Q: Is it true you can't walk?
A: Well, yeah, I suppose we hop instead. Or maybe it's a jump really, 'cause we keep our feet together. Anyway, we are VERY springy.

Q: That's true. How far can you jump?
A: 25 feet? 30? I don't really care!

Q: Wow, thirty feet is as long as a small bus! What else are kangaroos good at?
A: Oh, wrestling mainly.

SCRITCH SCRATCH

THUMP THUMP THUMP

Q: Wrestling? What do you wrestle? Other animals?
A: Oh no, mate, we don't worry about them. OK, now and again a dingo or a big eagle will try to grab our kids for lunch, but mostly they leave us alone 'cause we're big and fast. No, fella, I'm talking about wrestling other roos.

Q: Why do you do that?
A: You sure ask a lot of questions! We males fight over the females, y'know. We want to be daddies. Well, actually we want to be THE DADDY, the boss, the BIG K.

Q: But don't you get beaten up?
A: Yeah, sure, it's all part of life. We grab, we claw, and we kick hard with two feet to show who's toughest.

Q: Uh, this may be a daft question, but if you kick with two feet, don't you fall over?
A: You're right.

Q: What, you do fall over?
A: No, it was a daft question. We balance on our tails when we fight—they're mega strong.

Q: Ah, I see. Uh, it's often REALLY hot here in Australia, so how do you survive?
A: Yeah, some of us live in the desert, where it's hotter than a volcano's belly . . . So we stay in the shade during the daytime and go out and about later when the sun sets. It's much cooler then.

Q: What do you eat?
A: Plants, grass mainly.

Q: Well, that was a quick answer! Uh, what can you tell me about female kangaroos?
A: They're smaller than us, maybe half the weight? Then they have a pouch, of course . . .

Q: A what?
A: A pouch, where the joey stays when it's little.

Q: Joey? Is he your best pal?
A: Oh boy, I need to do a LOT of explaining . . . OK, listen hard. A joey is a baby kangaroo. When they are born, they are teeny little red things, smaller than a grape!

Q: You're kidding! Aren't you?
A: No, s'true! The teeny joey climbs into the mother's pouch where it can suckle—drink milk, y'know.

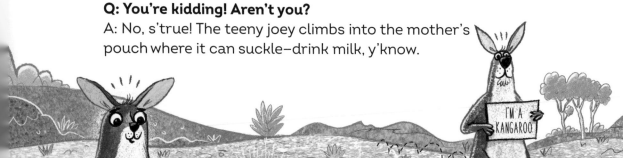

Q: And the pouch is . . . ?
A: It's like a big warm pocket on mom's tum. The joey stays in there for months while it's growing—for protection. They're cuter than pickles when their little heads pop out.

Q: Amazing! Are there any dangers for kangaroos? There seem to be a lot of you around.
A: Right, there's maybe 50 million of us in Oz—a lot more than humans! But yeah, there are still plenty of dangers—wildfires, droughts when it doesn't rain for AGES, farmers with guns, snakes, and then there's the big killer . . .

Q: The big killer?
A: Cars and trucks when we cross the road. Nasty.

Q: Oh dear, let's change the subject. What do you think of wallabies?
A: I think they're a LOT smaller than us. And not as fast. But they're harmless enough.

Q: Thank you, Mr. K.
A: OK, good, now hop to it.

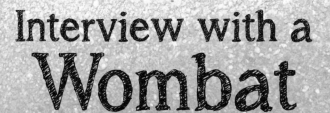

Interview with a
Wombat

My next interview is with a cuddly creature who
has little legs, a big bottom, and lots of surprises.
It's the wacky and wonderful . . . WOMBAT!

**Q: If you could sum up what it's like to be a
wombat in one word, what would it be?**
A: Pardon.

Q: If you could sum up–oh, hang on, was "pardon" your word?
A: Yes, we say it a lot. Mainly because we have, uh,
quite a lot of um, wind.

**Q: Oh, right, I thought it was a door creaking somewhere . . .
Anyway, can you tell me a few other things about yourself?**
A: We live in the forests and hills of Australia. We are
strong, quite fast, and very good diggers.

Q: So did you make all these burrows with your claws?
A: That's right, over 160 feet of tunnels
and chambers. Not bad, eh?

Q: Wow, there must be room for lots of wombats in there!
A: No, just me–we mostly spend time on our own.

Q: I thought you lived in groups?
A: No, no, no. You're thinking of hairy-nosed wombats. I'm a bare-nosed wombat, see?

Q: OK, I see, you do have a bare nose—and big teeth too. What are they for?
A: Amazingly, they are for eating.

Q: Haha, whoops, of course. What do you eat?
A: A lot of grass, but bark and roots too. You need tough teeth for those.

Q: And someone told me you have a tough backside too. Is that true?
A: Sure is. A big strong bottom like this helps defend us against dingoes—those horrible wild dogs.

CHOMP
CHOMP

**Q: Oh wow, there seems to be, well, a HEAD
sticking out of your bottom too!**
A: That's not my BOTTOM, that's my POUCH.
And she's my little baby. Hmphhh.

**Q: OH, you're a MOM, I see . . . But why is your pouch at the back?
A kangaroo's is at the front.**
A: Easy—to keep it from filling with soil when we dig.
The kid doesn't want a bunch of dirt in his mush!

**Q: I see—very clever! And on the subject of rear ends—sorry—
is it true that wombats poop is square?**
A: I was waiting for that question. Yes, it's true . . . Dice-
shaped droppings, cubic doo-doo, square squits,
perpendicular plops, blocky botty-bombs—IT'S TRUE!

Q: Right, OK! Why?
A: Simple: they don't roll away. We leave piles of them
to mark our territory and keep other wombats away.
I pop out about a hundred smelly cubes a night.

12

**Q: Whoa, but let's talk about something else . . .
What do you think of human beings?**
A: Let's face it, you're ANNOYING. You take up too much space, so we have less room to live and find food. And we're scared of you. That's why we sometimes knock you down or bite.

Q: Ooh, sorry. Our bad. You won't bite me, will you?
A: It depends if you annoy me in another way.

Q: Like what?
A: Like by telling that REALLY BAD wombat joke.

Q: What, you mean, "What's a wombat for?"
A: YES! Grrrrrrr!

Q: Sorry, sorry, sorry, it slipped out. Do you think we should tell them?
A: Who?

Q: The readers—tell them what a wombat is for?
A: Oh all right. It's for playing wom. Hil-ar-i-ous.

Q: I think I might just go now. Byee!
A: Good riddance.

Interview with an
Opossum

For this next interview I am not in Australia, I'm in the US and hoping to speak to the only marsupial found there. She's about the size of a pet cat, looks a little like a giant rat, and she's called the NORTH AMERICAN OPOSSUM.

Q: Hello, sorry to interrupt your dinner. Do you mind if I ask you a few questions?
A: Who are you? What do you want?

Q: I'm writing a book about animals and I'd like to interview you. Is that OK?
A: Hmmm, maybe. Most humans just call me a pest and shoo me away.

Q: Why's that?
A: I dunno, ask yourself!

Q: Uh, what are you eating?
A: Some pizza crust, if you must know.

HEY, IT'S MY TURN FOR THE FRONT SEAT.

Q: Wow, do opossums get takeout?
A: No, course not. I found it in a garbage can next to that house over there.

Q: Ah, the can that's been knocked over. It was someone's food waste put out for recycling, was it?
A: What are you talking about, strange man? It's just good eating, that's all.

Q: What else do you eat?
A: This and that. Fruit, eggs, worms, beetles, fish, carrots, mice, frogs, nuts, berries, snakes, and dead things mainly.

Q: So you're a scavenger, then?
A: A what? We eat what we can find. We clean things up—we're good!

Q: Are those your babies on your back?
A: Congratulations, I see you're a detective as well as a writer . . .

Q: Don't they fall off?
A: Nah, they've got a strong grip. And when they're little they stay in my pouch.

Q: I see. They're very cute, but what's the downside of being an opossum?
A: Besides interviews? Avoiding traffic on roads is hard. Then there are bloodthirsty predators out there: hawks, dogs, coyotes, bobcats, and foxes, for a start.

Q: What do you do if one of those attacks you? Um, you don't look very fast.
A: Hey, WATCH IT! We can run fast when we need to. We're great climbers, too—we can grip things with our tail.

Q: I heard that you sometimes play dead. Is that true?
A: Well, we don't exactly PLAY dead—it just sort of happens if we get a sudden fright.

Q: Please explain. What do you do?
A: It's like fainting. We just drop to the ground, lie still, and stare, with our mouth open and tongue out. We look like we've croaked.

Q: Does that fool predators?
A: It can, especially if we produce THE SMELL.

Q: What smell?
A: A kind of foul "dead-thing" stink comes out of our butt.

**Q: Ugh, I know humans who can do that . . .
Anyway, can I ask a couple more things?**
A: If you must . . .

**Q: I read somewhere that opossums have 50 teeth,
a small brain, and usually live for less than
two years. Are those things true?**
A: 50 teeth? I never counted! Small brain? I don't
understand the question. And living for two years?
I feel perfectly . . . ooh, ow, argh, urrgghh . . .

**Q: Mrs. Opossum? Are you OK? Say something!
Oh dear, what shall I do? Maybe she's pretending . . .
But what if she's dead? Are you dead?**
A: Yes.

Q: WHAT IS THAT SMELL?!
A: Hehehe . . .

17

Interview with a
Sugar Glider

This guest is simply a sensation. He may only be the size of a small squirrel, but he can fly! (Well, sort of.) All the way from the tropical forests of New Guinea, I bring you the SUGAR GLIDER!

Q: Is it true you can fly?
A: What? No, not really! We glide, we glide!

Q: Ah, that must be why you're called a glider. But where are your wings?
A: Wings? WINGS! I'm not a BIRD or a BAT! Come on . . . And I'm not a squirrel either. I'm a kind of possum with stretchy flaps of skin between my front and back legs, see?

Q: Oh yes, sorry—it's like a little parachute. So where do you glide?
A: Where? Where? In the trees! We live in forests. I have cousins in Indonesia and Australia, and we all leap from tree to tree, especially if we are being CHASED.

Q: What chases you?
A: Bad things! Horrible things. Predators! Owls grab us, lizards snatch us, snakes bite us, and cats and kookaburras eat us too if they can—I hate them!

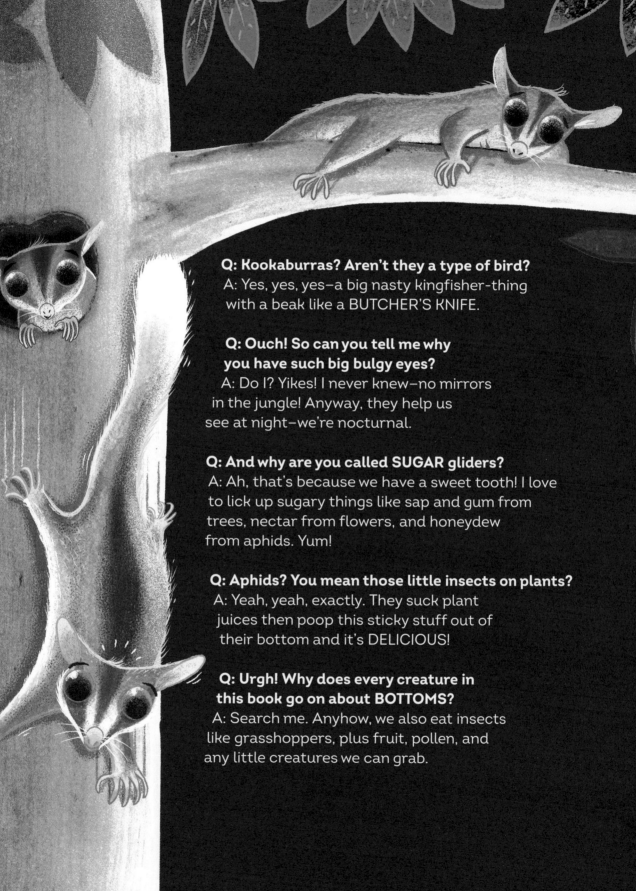

Q: Kookaburras? Aren't they a type of bird?
A: Yes, yes, yes–a big nasty kingfisher-thing
with a beak like a BUTCHER'S KNIFE.

**Q: Ouch! So can you tell me why
you have such big bulgy eyes?**
A: Do I? Yikes! I never knew–no mirrors
in the jungle! Anyway, they help us
see at night–we're nocturnal.

Q: And why are you called SUGAR gliders?
A: Ah, that's because we have a sweet tooth! I love
to lick up sugary things like sap and gum from
trees, nectar from flowers, and honeydew
from aphids. Yum!

Q: Aphids? You mean those little insects on plants?
A: Yeah, yeah, exactly. They suck plant
juices then poop this sticky stuff out of
their bottom and it's DELICIOUS!

**Q: Urgh! Why does every creature in
this book go on about BOTTOMS?**
A: Search me. Anyhow, we also eat insects
like grasshoppers, plus fruit, pollen, and
any little creatures we can grab.

Q: So you're an omnivore?
A: Whatever. Next question!

Q: OK, right. Are you a loner or a family guy?
A: Come on, do I look like a loner? Pah, NO WAY! We gliders like to stick together—we LOVE each other's company.

Q: Even the males like you?
A: Yeah, bro, EVEN THE MALES LIKE ME. I help look after the kids and everything. My family group is just so CLOSE, you know. Love 'em.

Q: What about other sugar gliders from other groups around you?
A: What? Them? Oh, they'd better watch out! They'd better not come near our territory or it's BAM! And KERPOW! And MUNCH! If they don't have my scent, they can GET LOST!

Q: Oooh, I see. Did you know that some people keep sugar gliders as pets? Even though they are very hard to care for?
A: What! Really? In CAGES? Gah, I would HATE to be kept indoors in some human's smelly house. Nightmare!

Q: But you are very cute—and you can glide, maybe that's why it happens?
A: Probably. But listen, I would bite anyone who tried to put me in a cage: SNAP!

Q: Can you tell me anything else about you?
A: Sure, sure. We are amazing climbers, for one. Oh yes, and this: I come from a warm rainforest, but some gliders live in cooler places. When it gets cold, they all huddle together in a furry ball to stay warm. Sweet, no?

Q: Thank you, that's been very interesting.
A: Truly? OK, cool. Just make sure the illustrator makes me look really good!

Interview with a
Koala

Now for a special treat. This is one of the world's cutest and most popular animals. It's another star of the Australian bush—it's the One. And. Only. KOALA!

Q: Many people say you look like a teddy bear. Are you a bear?
A: No.

Q: Good, that's cleared that up, then. So what kind of creature are you?
A: I see you have much to learn, oh beardy one. We are what we are: slow, wise, gentle guardians of the trees.

Q: Right. Why do you spend all your time up there among the branches?
A: The higher you are, the farther you see. Here we find peace, rest, and solitude.

Q: Anything else?
A: Yes, tons of leaves to scoff.

Q: Is it true that you only eat leaves of eucalyptus trees?
A: Indeed. The gum tree is our heaven. It gives us all we need—food, shelter, and safety.

Q: Do you ever fall out?
A: With each other or the trees?

Q: Uh, both?
A: We are solitary beings—we prefer to be alone, so we avoid other koalas, unless to mate. We rarely fall from trees, even in high winds, but it can happen. Hurts like anything.

Q: So, how do you grip branches strongly in a storm?
A: Ah yes, our paws are special. I am the owner of six thumbs.

Q: Wow! Did you know we only have two?
A: Of course. That is why I would advise you not to live in a tree.

Q: You're known to sleep for up to twenty hours a day. Why is that?
A: Well, the answer is simple. Eucalyptus trees are not rich food. We rest to save energy.

Q: If you could change the world, what would you do?
A: Ah, what a question . . . I would not seek such power, for that which benefits us may harm others.

Q: Oh, go on—you can tell me one thing, can't you?
A: Very well. I would wish for more trees.

Q: Why's that?
A: So our species can survive. Our numbers have fallen greatly. In the days of my ancestors there were twenty times more koalas in these lands.

Q: What happened?
A: Men came, men with guns.

Q: You were hunted?
A: Killed for our fur and for meat. But you humans have been cutting down the forests for centuries too. You should plant more and chop less.

Q: I agree. But at least today most humans love you. That is something good, isn't it?
A: Yes, we feel your warmth. We are glad for the nature reserves you make too.

SNORE

Q: What else is important to you?
A: We fear the long dry summers and forest fires and traffic and dogs.

**Q: And what do you value,
besides the trees?**
A: The colors of the sunset, the song of the hills, the caress of a baby . . .

Q: Do you have any children?
A: There is one in my pouch. Come out and say hello, little one.

Q: Oh, he is GORGEOUS. So sweet!
A: Thank you. It's a she.

Q: Is it time to leave you in peace?
A: That would be best. Farewell, writer man. Plant trees, guard the earth, and don't wear purple and brown together.

Interview with a Quokka

What a delight it is to talk to my next marsupial guest. Known as the "the happiest animal in the world," she is about the size of a large rabbit and just as adorable. Here is the one and only QUOKKA!

Q: Hi! Do you mind if I take a selfie with you?
A: Everyone wants a selfie with me! You humans are OBSESSED with them! Why?

Q: Um, it's because you're the happiest animal on Earth! Aren't you?
A: No, I am not.

Q: Oh dear. Why not?
A: Because two-legged twerps keep asking for selfies!

Q: Oh sorry, it's just that your little smile is so cute . . .
A: That's not a smile, it's just the way we look. Oh how I wish it wasn't . . .

Q: Whoops. It sounds more like you're the saddest animal on Earth.
A: Well, maybe that's because there are too many people on this island. I just want to be LEFT IN PEACE.

SPLOS

Q: Sorry. Can I ask you just one thing?
A: What?

Q: This little island you live on near Australia–why is it called Rottnest?
A: It's because some Dutch sea captain, who sailed here
hundreds of years ago, thought we were giant rats.

Q: And are you?
A: No we are NOT. The nerve! Quokkas are more like wallabies.

Q: So that man thought this island was a rat's nest?
A: Yeah, another twerp. We like it here because
there are no foxes, cats, or dogs.

Q: What do they do?
A: Oh, not much, only
kill us a bit . . .

I'M LIVID.

Q: Ah, is that why there are not many quokkas left in Australia?
A: Partly. But mainly it's you guys. You cut down trees, make farms, and build houses in the places we used to live. And you sometimes cause bush fires.

Q: Sorry, again. I seem to spend a lot of time saying that. Is it hard to escape the humans here on the island?
A: Sometimes. But often we sleep during the day among the prickly bushes where you can't go. And if people try to pet us, we can bite.

Q: OK, no cuddles! What do you usually eat, by the way?
A: Not fish and chips like you guys. Juicy plants—fresh salad!

Q: I notice you're chewing now—why's that?
A: Oh, it's just some grass I swallowed earlier. We can bring it back up and chew it again. It helps us digest our food.

Q: Right, uh, nice. What else can you do?
A: Climb trees. Well, we can a little.

Q: Do you have any kids?
A: One small joey in my pouch, having a feed on my milk. I have two each year.

Q: Wow, so how many babies have you had altogether?
A: Sixteen.

Q: Amazing! This island must be a safe place to raise a family?
A: Well, there are still dangerous snakes here, and some quokkas become ill when HUMANS try to feed them junk food.

Q: Oh no, I'd better say sorry AGAIN!
A: Yes, you should.

Q: OK, that's about it. Were you happy with the interview?
A: Yes, I suppose so.

Q: So you ARE happy sometimes?
A: Now and again. Mainly when interviews are over!

Interview with a Numbat

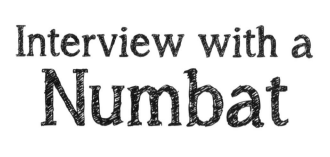

Up next is one of the world's rarest animals. He is found only in Australia and looks like an inflated striped squirrel. It is the gorgeous NUMBAT!

Q: Welcome! How are you?
A: Who are you? You're not a giant numbat, are you?

Q: No, I'm not a numbat. No tail or striped fur, see? And numbats don't wear pants.
A: Ah yes, that's true. Well, it's a GOOD JOB you're not— we don't like other numbats coming into our territory.

Q: Why's that?
A: Why? WHY? They'll eat our food or fight us for starters! How would you like it if some big hairy guy just walked into your house, noshed all your cheese, and bopped you on the noggin?

Q: Ah, I see. So where do you live?
A: In holes and hollow logs. But there are not many of us left now.

Q: Oh dear. I read about that. Can you tell me why numbats are endangered?
A: Yes, it's sad. There are less than a thousand of us left in the wild. It's mainly because of foxes and cats.

Q: Oh dear. Do they . . . are they . . . ?
A: Bogheads? Yes.

Q: I thought it would be hawks and snakes that were your main predators?
A: Well, they do catch us as well, it's true. But we are good at spotting those animals. Foxes and cats are not native to Australia.

Q: What do you mean?
A: They were brought here by outsiders—by people from Europe. The cats and foxes spread all over the country, and now they kill a LOT of wild animals. They are clever hunters.

Q: Oh those silly people! Anyway, let's change the subject to something more cheerful. What do you enjoy doing?
A: Eating termites. In fact, they are all we eat.

Q: What, those little insects that look like ants?
A: Yes. They are softer and juicier than ants. I eat about 15,000 a day. Yum yum!

Q: Ah, so do you have a long tongue like an anteater then?
A: Correct. And sticky spit. Also, we don't have proper teeth because we don't chew.

Q: But termites live underground. How do you know where to dig?
A: We have excellent eyesight and a very good sense of smell. We can spot their nests.

Q: So you must go out searching during the day. Don't most marsupials come out at night?
A: That's right. Sadly, it's another reason why predators catch us so easily. Life stinks sometimes . . . How do *you* avoid being eaten?

Q: Me? Oh, I stay FAR away from lions, sharks, monsters, and cannibals. Plus, I have a pair of camouflage socks.
A: Hmmmm.

Q: A few more questions. Do you live in a family group?
A: No, we live alone. I do have some kids somewhere,
I think. We male numbats are not very good fathers . . .

Q: Where's their mother?
A: Uh, somewhere over there. Or there. Possibly.

Q: Can you tell me anything about female numbats?
A: Of course. They have four tiny babies a year,
just three-quarters of an inch long when
born. Plus, they don't have a pouch.

Q: What? WHATTT! I thought all marsupials have pouches?
A: Calm down, calm down. No, they don't.

**Q: Right, wow. So what do you think of humans? I guess
you probably hate us because of the cat and fox thing?**
A: No, not really. Those settlers didn't know what they were
doing. Yes, humans have destroyed a lot of our woodland
habitats, but many have also done good things for us.

Q: Like what?
A: Like protecting us with fences, making nature
reserves, and breeding numbats in zoos.

Q: Whew! Finally, what is your favorite kind of music?
A: Anything by the White Stripes.

LET'S PLAY HIDE
AND SQUEAK.

Interview with a Tasmanian devil

And now prepare yourselves to meet a dark,
menacing animal with a fearsome name. It's smelly,
it's loud, it's bitey—it's the TASMANIAN DEVIL!

Q: Would you mind telling me why you are called a devil?
A: Can I just say what a surprise it is to meet
you here in Tazzie. I have all your books.

Q: Oh, thank you.
A: I'm just kidding about that. I've actually never heard of you.

**Q: Right, I'm starting to think I might know why you're
called a devil . . .**
A: I like your hat. It's a shame that's the type that redbacks like
to crawl into—y'know, those very deadly spiders we have here.

Q: I'm going to ignore that. Since you won't answer questions, perhaps you can just tell me if these things are true or not?
A: False! Okay, okay, go on.

Q: Are you the largest marsupial carnivore?
A: True.

Q: Can you really bite through bones and even wire?
A: True.

Q: Do you live all over Australia?
A: Oh, this is SO BORING. All right, all right, I'll tell you some things. But you'll be SHOCKED.

Q: Yesss! Where shall we start?
A: OK, well, we live on the island of Tasmania, although there are a few of us in mainland Australia now too.

Q: And why are you called a devil?
A: We can't all be goody-goodies, ha! No, it's because some sailors in olden times heard us screeching, like something evil. We squeal and growl a lot when fighting over food.

Q: What kind of food?
A: Oh, we hunt for all kind of stuff and eat whatever we can find: possums, wombats, wallabies, frogs, snakes, birds, insects, eggs, and dead stuff.

Q: Dead stuff?
A: Yeah, y'know—roadkill or any animal that's croaked in the wild.

Q: People tell me that you like to pig out. Is that right?
A: How rude! They can get lost.

Q: But it's true, isn't it?
A: Well, yes, it's true, but it's just the way we are. We love food! If I find a body and I'm hungry, I'll scoff the whole thing: meat, guts, organs, bones, even fur. If it's a big creature, five or six of us join in, ripping it to pieces. It's FUN!

Q: Doesn't that make you sick sometimes?
A: Nah, it makes us POOP a lot, though. We like to go to the bathroom together. Yeah, some of my plops are eight inches long!

Q: What's the bad side of being a Tasmanian devil?
A: Right, well, being hit by cars where we're munching roadkill isn't great. We also suffer from NASTY diseases. And we don't live long—maybe four to five years. Most Taz kiddies don't live long, either.

Q: What do you mean?
A: Females give birth to loads of really teeny babies, maybe 25. Each one weighs about the same as a RAINDROP.

Q: Wow, what happens to them?
A: They have to crawl over their mother to her pouch to feed and grow. But there are only four teats in there, so . . .

Q: Oh dear. Let's lighten the mood. What's good about being a devil?
A: Now you are TALKING! Well, apart from all the EATING, we are kind of the top dudes on Taz—there are no dingoes on the island to get us, so we rule!

Q: So how come you are endangered animals?
A: Well mate, you DAFT HUMANS used to think we ate all your sheep, so you tried to DO AWAY with us. But now our numbers are low because of illnesses. We don't have devil doctors, nurses, or ambulances . . .

Q: I'm sure that people are trying to help you survive now, though. Aren't they?
A: Yeah, true, you're not ALL bad.

Q: Thank you.
A: I'm not sure about you, though.

OKAY BELLA, YOU WIN POOP OF THE DAY.

Interview with a
CUSCUS

Now you have a chance to meet another shy and rarely seen marsupial. Found on the tropical island of New Guinea, this cat-sized creature is the COMMON SPOTTED CUSCUS!

Q: Hello, have you ever been interviewed before?
A: Hello. This is my first ever interview and I am quite nervous.

Q: Don't worry, you'll be fine! What's it like living in a rainforest?
A: Uh, yes, well, it's both good and bad, really.

Q: Why good?
A: Well, there is plenty of food for us, such as leaves, shoots, and fruit, as well as small animals to catch. And the trees help us hide too.

Q: Hide from what?
A: Ooh, I was afraid you'd ask that. We have to watch out for big snakes–pythons–and eagles too. We try to stay hidden in the day.

Q: Do you sleep in the trees?
A: Yes, we spend almost all our time in them. To sleep we make a little platform out of branches, and we sometimes cover ourselves with leaves for camouflage.

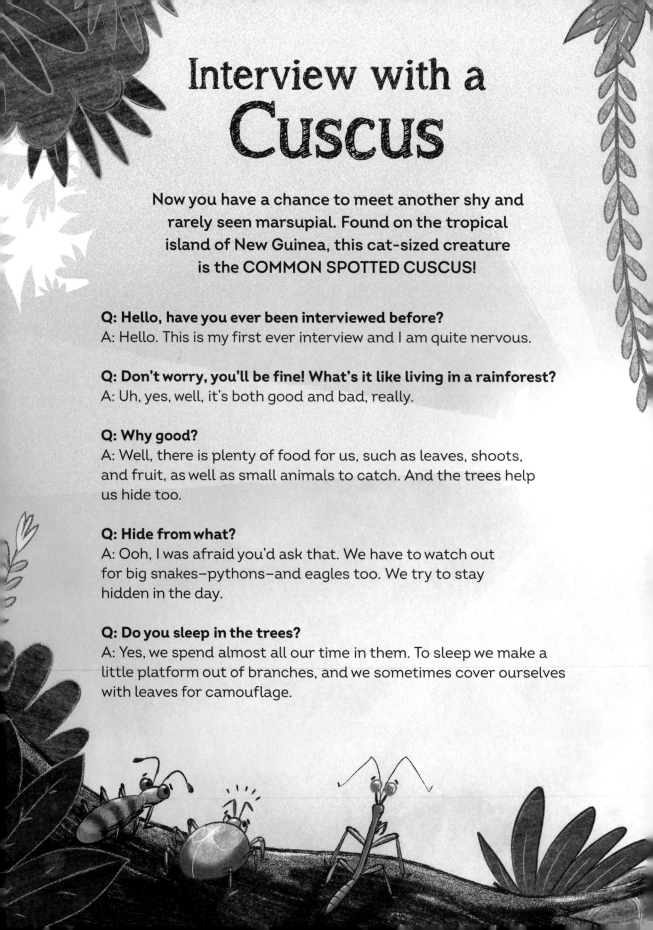

Q: Smart! So you mainly feed at night? Is that why you have those big eyes?
A: Yes, partly. We are most active at dawn and dusk, really.

Q: You must be good climbers then?
A: A cuscus has to be. We have strong claws, but also a special tail with scales on it to grip branches.

Q: Are you a male or a female?
A: I'm a female. We have plain white or grayish fur, while males are spotted and have different colors. Our young change color as they grow—they can be red, white, brown, tan, gray, or even black.

Q: Amazing. Do you have a pouch?
A: Yes, indeed. Like other marsupials, we give birth to tiny babies that have been growing inside us for only a few weeks. They grow further in the pouch.

YOU SMELL.

Q: Ah, is that what is special about marsupials?
A: Correct.

Q: I notice you're alone. Do cuscus not live in groups?
A: Oh, no, no, no. We are solitary, especially the males. They keep well apart, or fights break out.

Q: Fights? But you look so gentle, and you move so slowly.
A: True, but males will hiss, scratch, bite, and kick to defend their territory.

Q: But how does one cuscus know which part of the forest is another's territory?
A: Ooh, these are very hard questions. It's like having a test at school!

Q: Sorry, I'm just really interested. Do you know the answer?
A: Of course. They leave their stinky scent. They rub against trees and also spit on branches. Every animal's scent is different, so others can sniff the warning.

Q: Ah, I see. We humans have a very poor sense of smell compared with most animals, but we are better at puzzles.
A: At what?

Q: Uh, nothing . . . I wish I hadn't said that.
A: Is this part of the interview?

Q: No, not really, I'm just babbling.
A: You're very strange. I think I'll be on my way now . . .

NO, YOU SMELL!

Interview with a
Bandicoot

I now have the pleasure of speaking to a rabbit-sized animal from Australia that many people have heard of but some think isn't real. She is! Please give a special welcome to the BANDICOOT!

Q: I hope you don't mind me asking—why do you have such a long nose?
A: Why do YOU have such a funny chin?

Q: Um, hang on, I'm supposed to be asking the questions!
A: Why?

Q: Well, I'm the interviewer, that's why. So about your nose?
A: What about it?

Q: Why is it so long?
A: Do you REALLY need to know? OK, OK, it's because I'm a LONG-NOSED bandicoot, that's why. There are also short-nosed bandicoots, spiny bandicoots, pygmy bandicoots, striped bandicoots, golden bandicoots, and rabbit-eared bandicoots. Happy?

Q: Wow, lots of bandicoots. I'm guessing your nose helps you find food?
A: What does your chin help you find?

Q: Um, well, uh... Hey, you're asking all the questions again! Can you answer some please?
A: How many?

Q: Hmmm. OK, try this: is there anything you would like to change about your life?
A: What did you say? All right, only kidding! Changes? Yes, I would like an INVISIBLE FORCE FIELD to stop owls swooping down on me, and dingoes grabbing me for their dinner. AND, I'd like worms, beetles, grubs, spiders, and caterpillars to always crawl towards me, so I don't have to spend ALL NIGHT searching and digging for them. Plus, someone to bring me some mushrooms and plants to nibble.

Q: So you're nocturnal?
A: Noc-what?

Q: It means you're active a night.
A: Of course, why wouldn't we be? Duh! In the day there are too many DANGERS about. Bandicoots like the cover of darkness.

Q: Where do you sleep?
A: Where do *you* sleep?

Q: In a bed.
A: So do I. But mine's more like a nest made of grass and leaves. Did you know that?

Q: I do now! Do you spend time with other bandicoots?
A: Why would I do THAT?

Q: Uh, maybe to make friends or to start a family?
A: Do you mind, that's PERSONAL! We spend almost all of our time ALONE and prefer it that way. But yes, we do need to have babies or there will be NO MORE BANDICOOTS. That would be bad, sad, terrible, shocking, horrible, dreadful, disastrous, annoying, stinky, and GAH. I would be FURIOUS!

I WISH I'D LEARNED KARATE.

Q: I agree, so how can humans help you?
A: Are you offering? Anything? I'd like some soup and a new hat. No, really, you can help by NOT DOING STUFF.

Q: Ooh. What kind of things?
A: Isn't it obvious? Things that CHANGE THE BALANCE OF NATURE. I mean stuff like destroying the bush, poisoning the air with motor fumes, cutting down trees, and letting animals into Australia that DON'T BELONG HERE. Get the idea?

Q: I see. We don't want any more bandicoots to become extinct. Or any other animals. Let's try to end on something cheerful. Do you have a fun fact about bandicoots to share?
A: Why not? OK, two of our toes on our back feet are joined together. We use them like combs.

Q: Thank you!
A: You can go now.

45

How you can help

It was fun meeting those animals, wasn't it? But some of them are NOT HAPPY because they are losing their homes or having trouble finding food or meeting horrible traffic.

The sad thing is that a lot of this is because of us. We humans hog so much of the Earth, making some of the creatures in this book ENDANGERED.

Australia has already lost some animals forever, like the Tasmanian tiger. It's now EXTINCT. We can stop this from happening again by taking better care of our planet.

1. Get active
The more time you spend outdoors in nature, the better you understand it. Ask if you can do some of these:
- Explore a forest—see what you can spot in the woods
- Visit a nature reserve
- Explore a park you haven't been to
- Walk along the banks of a river—stick to the trail!

2. Join a local group
There are groups of people everywhere who work to care for the environment. Many organizations that protect animals offer activities and clubs for children, such as your local Audubon Society.

3. Be a walker or cyclist
A lot of animals suffer because there are too many cars on the roads:
- Walk for short trips—try not to go by car
- Learn to ride safely on the roads by bike—take a cycling class
- Get in shape by walking, riding, and jogging. You'll be healthier and feel better!
- Take care when crossing roads. Adults know the safest places to cross.

4. Raise money

Nature organizations depend on money to do important conservation work, protecting the wildlife that is under threat. Here's how you can help them:

- 🌿 Adopt an endangered animal with World Wildlife Fund or a similar group
- 🌿 Ask a teacher if your school can help with raising money for wildlife
- 🌿 Find out about smaller nonprofits that help animals, such as the cuscus and wombat

5. Help prevent pollution

Making and using most things involves energy and can create nasty pollution. Vehicles add to climate change too, and all of this affects wild animals. Here are some ways to REDUCE pollution:

- 🌿 Turn off lights when you're not using them
- 🌿 Unplug chargers
- 🌿 Switch off devices when you're finished with them
- 🌿 Reuse and recycle as much as possible
- 🌿 Don't litter

6. Avoid using plastic

We now know that tiny pieces of plastic are getting into oceans, rivers, soil, and more. This is not good for animals!

- 🌿 Instead of plastic bags, use any bag that can be used several times
- 🌿 For drinks, use a bottle that can be refilled
- 🌿 Use bars of soap instead of shower gel in plastic bottles

7. Tell our leaders

It's up to the people in charge to make changes that help wildlife. You can encourage them by writing letters that show you care about protecting wild animals and their habitats. Ask a parent or guardian how to do this.

8. Learn more

This book has helped you understand a little about the lives of some special animals. Use your local library (where the books are free to borrow) to find out more and to discover what else you can do to protect OUR AMAZING PLANET.

Quiz

Can you answer these fun questions about each of the ten marsupials in the book? All the information is on the pages somewhere. Answers are at the bottom of this page.

1. What is a baby kangaroo called?
a) A gooey   b) A joey   c) A pouchy   d) Desmond

2. What does a wombat use to defend itself against dingoes?
a) Its bottom   b) Its teeth   c) Its claws   d) A baseball bat

3. How does an opossum sometimes fool predators?
a) By hiding   b) By looking like a log
c) By playing dead   d) By dressing as a wolf

4. Sugar gliders eat honeydew, which comes from where?
a) Melons   b) Flowers   c) The Internet   d) Aphids' bottoms

5. How many thumbs does a koala have?
a) 4   b) 6   c) 0   d) 237

6. What do quokkas eat?
a) Insects   b) Plants   c) Foxes   d) Pizza

7. How big is a baby numbat when born?
a) 3/4 in.   b) 3/100 in.   c) 3 ft.   d) 3 mi.

8. Why are Tasmanian devils called devils?
a) They have horns   b) They are very evil
c) They have red eyes   d) They screech a lot

9. What does a cuscus do during the day?
a) Hunts   b) Digs burrows   c) Sleeps a lot   d) Goes shopping

10. What does a bandicoot use to groom its fur?
a) A comb   b) A stick   c) Toes   d) Curling iron

Answers: 1b 2a 3c 4d 5b 6b 7a 8d 9c 10c